# Image of the

# SOLDIER

A Photographic History of The Durham Light Infantry

from the Crimean War to the Final Parade.

COUNTY DURHAM BOOKS

**Front cover:**
DRO D/DLI 2/1/280(340)

**Back cover (top to bottom):**
DRO D/DLI 2/7/18(1)
DRO D/DLI 7/805 (155)
DRO D/DLI 7/14/1
DRO D/DLI 2/1/541
DRO D/DLI 2/2/148(199)

The photographs in this volume are part of the Durham Light Infantry Collection [D/DLI] held in the Durham County Record Office. The photographs were selected by, and the commentary was written by, members of staff of the Durham County Record Office and the Durham Light Infantry Museum.

Published by County Durham Books, 2005

County Durham Books is the imprint of **Durham County Council**, Culture & Leisure

✆ 0191 383 4479  www.durham.gov.uk/countydurhambooks

ISBN 1-897585-82-9

# FOREWORD

Henry Sladden survived, when so many men of the 68th Regiment of Foot died from fighting and disease in the Crimea; he had not a day's illness during the long years of war. After the campaign he continued to serve, finally ending his days terrorising young recruits at the Regimental Depot in Sunderland.

When you look at one of the earliest photographs of the 68th Light Infantry- the ancestor of The Durham Light Infantry - taken during the Crimean War your eye is drawn to a splendidly bearded soldier wearing The Distinguished Conduct Medal. At the time this was the sole gallantry award available to Non Commissioned ranks and the soldier was Henry Sladden himself

Men like Henry Sladden were the foundation of The Durham Light Infantry and this book of photographs, selected from thousands now held in the Durham Record Office, will introduce you to many of them who served and fought across the world from the cold trenches outside Sebastopol to the jungle-covered mountains of Borneo. You will see these soldiers on parade, in their barrack rooms, in the trenches, playing football, in prison camps and even relaxing with a beer. The book is further enriched as you look into the world of their families; the women and children who so loyally followed the 'Durhams', and their man, around the world from the dust of India to the glamour of Hong Kong.

"Image of the Soldier" is a superb book full of outstanding photographs that capture the spirit of The Durham Light Infantry, an outstanding County Regiment remembered and renowned to this day for its courageous record in war throughout the past 150 years. Looking at these photographs, I feel pride and gratitude that I too was fortunate enough to serve over some 40 years with so many fine people in one of our Nation's finest fighting Regiments.

**General Sir Peter de la Billière** KCB, KBE, DSO, MC*, DL

**1** Soldiers of the 68th Light Infantry in the Crimea in April 1855.
Standing (third from right) is Sergeant Henry Sladden, who is
wearing his recently awarded Distinguished Conduct Medal.

DRO D/DLI 2/1/299(1)

CRIMEAN WAR

**2** Soldiers of the 68th Light Infantry wearing their winter uniforms in the Crimea in April 1855. These are the same men as in photograph No. 1. These are two of the earliest known photographs of the Regiment.

**3** Born in 1821 at Tralee in Ireland, Thomas O'Leary served as the 68th Light Infantry's Surgeon during the Crimean War. This portrait was taken about 1858.

# CRIMEAN WAR

**4** Officers of the 68th Light Infantry in the Crimea on 19 May 1855. Standing (second from right) is Captain Thomas Hamilton, who had won the Victoria Cross a week earlier.

DRO D/DLI 2/1/298

CRIMEAN WAR

**5** Soldiers, bandsmen and boys of the 1st South Durham Militia
on parade in the Market Place, Barnard Castle, County Durham,
about 1855. This is possibly the earliest known photograph of this
Militia Regiment.

DRO D/DLI 2/4/318

COUNTY DURHAM

**6** A view of Rangoon taken about 1860. The 68th Light Infantry served in Burma on garrison duty from 1858 to 1863.

**7** A group of the 68th Light Infantry's officers - nicknamed the "Teetotallers" on the original photograph - relaxing at Thayetmyo in Burma, about 1860.

**BURMA**

**8** Officers of the newly-formed 4th Durham Rifle Volunteers in the garden of a house in the Market Place, Bishop Auckland, County Durham, about 1861.

DRO D/DLI 2/6/127(2)

**9** Lieutenant William Wilcox, 3rd Durham Rifle Volunteers at Whitburn, near Sunderland, about 1862. This photograph was taken by the Reverend C.L. Dodgson, better known as the author Lewis Carroll.

DRO D/DLI 2/7/18(1)

**10** Officers and soldiers of the 1st South Durham Militia at Barnard Castle, County Durham, about 1864. Born in 1787, Edward Nixon (centre in bicorn hat) was the Militia's Sur~ for 40 years.

DRO D/DLI 2/4/325

NEW ZEALAND

**11** Officers and soldiers of the 68th Light Infantry at Te Papa Camp in Tauranga, New Zealand, in April 1865, including their Commanding Officer, Colonel Henry Greer (seated third from left).

**12** The soldiers of the 68th Light Infantry who died in New Zealand were buried in the cemetery at Te Papa in Tauranga. This photograph was taken about 1866.

DRO D/DLI 2/1/307

NEW ZEALAND

**13** This portrait of Tomika Te Mutu, a Maori chief at Tauranga, New Zealand, was taken about 1866. He was famed for his moko (tattoos) on his face and body.

DRO D/DLI 7/409/9(239)

**14** Captain Aubrey Harvey Tucker, 68th Light Infantry, fought in both the Crimean and New Zealand Wars. This portrait was taken in Manchester in 1868.

DRO D/DLI 2/1/265(76)

# NEW ZEALAND

**15** The Band and Colours of the 106th Light Infantry at Umballa, India, about 1869. In 1881, this Regiment, originally part of the East India Company, became the 2nd Battalion DLI.

DRO D/DLI 2/2/153(1)

**16** Officers of the 2nd North Durham Militia on the steps of
Durham Castle about 1870. County Durham had two Militia
Regiments based in Barnard Castle and Durham.

DRO D/DLI 2/3/19

COUNTY DURHAM

**17** Permanent Staff Sergeants of the 2nd North Durham Militia
with their families outside the Militia Headquarters at Gilesgate,
Durham, about 1874.

COUNTY DURHAM

**18** This portrait of Colour Sergeant Ross of "C" Company 1st South Durham Fusiliers Militia was taken at Barnard Castle, County Durham, in 1870.

DRO D/DLI 2/4/310(77)

**19** This portrait of Captain and Adjutant Edward Agnew of the 1st South Durham Fusiliers Militia was taken at Redcar in Yorkshire, about 1874.

DRO D/DLI 2/4/310(28)

# COUNTY DURHAM

**20** With the Pioneers and Band at the front, the entire 68th Light Infantry is on parade here in India, about 1874. In 1881, this Regiment became the 1st Battalion DLI.

DRO D/DLI 2/1/319

INDIA

**21** The officers of the 68th Light Infantry at Poona in India in 1873. Crimean veteran Quartermaster Henry Sladden DCM (seated third from left) had first joined the 68th in 1845.

INDIA

**22** A cricket team of officers and soldiers from the 68th Light Infantry in India, about 1876. The 68th played cricket whenever it was possible, even in the Crimea and New Zealand.

DRO D/DLI 2/1/320

INDIA

**23** A group of officers and ladies from the 1st Battalion DLI prepares to hunt with a "bobbery" (mixed) pack of dogs at Allahabad, India, in December 1885.

DRO D/DLI 7/639/7

**INDIA**

**24** Officers of the newly-formed 2nd Battalion DLI at the Curragh Camp in Kildare, Ireland, in 1882 with the old Colours of the 106th Light Infantry.

DRO D/DLI 2/2/162(2)

**IRELAND**

**25** The Bugle Band of the 3rd Battalion DLI poses for a group photograph outside a barrack room at Colchester, Essex, in 1885 with (probably) the Bugle Major's wife and children.

DRO D/DLI 2/4/312(14)

ESSEX

**26** Between March and September 1885, these huts became the temporary home of the 3rd (Militia) Battalion DLI, when the battalion was sent to Colchester, Essex, as part of the garrison.

DRO D/DLI 2/4/312(27)

**27** These were the quarters of Lieutenant Sutton, whilst he was serving with the 3rd Battalion DLI at Colchester, Essex, in 1885.

DRO D/DLI 2/4/312(25)

ESSEX

**28** In 1885, while at Colchester Garrison, Essex, Band Sergeant
Kelly of the 3rd Battalion DLI got married. During this embodiment,
many of the part-time Militiamen had their families with them.

DRO D/DLI 2/4/312(17)

ESSEX

**29** A group of officers of the 3rd Battalion DLI pose in their mess dress outside one of the huts at Colchester Garrison, Essex, in 1885.

DRO D/DLI 2/4/312(8)

**30** A group of officers' servants from the 3rd Battalion DLI at Colchester Garrison, Essex, in 1885. Each officer had his own servant during this time at Colchester.

DRO D/DLI 2/4/312(12)

ESSEX

**31** On 1 January 1886, this Sudanese boy was found by the River Nile after the Battle of Ginnis, in the Sudan. Adopted by the 2nd Battalion DLI's Sergeants, he was known as "Jimmy Durham".

DRO D/DLI 7/194/1

EGYPT

INTER-REGIMENTAL POLO TOURNAMENT, 1896 and 1897.
WON BY 2nd BN. DURHAM LIGHT INFANTRY.

H. B. DES V. WILKINSON, 2.    D'A. W. MANDER    J. W. AINSWORTH, 1.
(Fifth Man).

H. DE B. DE LISLE, 3.                                    C. C. LUARD, Back.

**32** This is the 2nd Battalion DLI's team that won the Inter-Regimental Polo Cup in India in 1896 and 1897. Their Captain, Henry de Lisle (left), found Jimmy Durham in 1886.

DRO D/DLI 2/2/169

INDIA

**33** An officer of the 2nd Battalion DLI (right) with an Indian cavalryman on plague duty during an outbreak of bubonic plague in Poona, India, in April 1897.

DRO D/DLI 7/346/6

**INDIA**

**34** Soldiers from "B" Company 2nd Battalion DLI taking part in a bridge building competition in Burma, about 1899.

BURMA

**35** Soldiers from "H" Company 3rd Battalion DLI on musketry
practice at Deepdale, near Barnard Castle, County Durham,
about 1890.

DRO D/DLI 2/4/311(49)

**36** Officers of the 1st Battalion DLI with the Crown Prince of Siam (eighth from left) and his Aide de Camp, who were the battalion's guests at Aldershot, Hampshire, in 1899.

DRO D/DLI 7/654/1(2)

HAMPSHIRE

**37** The 1st Battalion DLI getting ready to board the *Cephalonia* at Southampton docks, on 24 October 1899, for the voyage to South Africa and the Boer War.

DRO D/DLI 7/654/1(3)

**38** A group of Non-Commissioned Officers of the 1st Battalion DLI on board the Cunard steamship *Cephalonia* en route for South Africa and the Boer War in late 1899.

DRO D/DLI 7/654/1(4)

# BOER WAR

**39** The 1st Battalion DLI marching through the small town of Estcourt in Natal, South Africa, in December 1899, towards the battle front on the Tugela River.

**40** Embodied in January 1900, the 4th (Militia) Battalion DLI was sent from Newcastle upon Tyne to Aldershot, Hampshire, as part of the garrison. Here the Militiamen are exercising with their rifles.

DRO D/DLI 2/3/17(3)

BOER WAR

**42** Soldiers of the 3rd (Militia) Battalion DLI about to move off aboard open-topped railway carriages in South Africa in May 1900.

DRO D/DLI 2/4/315(259)

**41** In January 1900, the 3rd Battalion DLI sailed for South Africa on board the *Umbria* - the first Militia unit to volunteer for the Boer War. Here, Militiamen relax on deck.

DRO D/DLI 2/4/315(30)

**43** Soldiers of "A" Company 3rd (Militia) Battalion DLI on active service in South Africa in 1900.

DRO D/DLI 2/4/315(190)

**BOER WAR**

**44** A fortified blockhouse in South Africa, near the bridge over the Orange River, manned from February to May 1902, by soldiers of "E" Company 4th (Militia) Battalion DLI.

DRO D/DLI 2/3/17(6)

**45** From 1901 to 1904, Wellington Barracks high in the Nilgiris
(Blue Mountains) in southern India was home, first to the 2nd
Battalion and then to the 1st Battalion DLI.

DRO D/DLI7/427/2(30)

INDIA

**46** A group of Boer Prisoners of War held at Wellington Barracks
in India and guarded by the DLI, circa. 1902

DRO D/DLI 7/427/2(23)

INDIA

**47** Here, the soldiers of "K" Company 1st Battalion DLI have decorated their room at Wellington Barracks in India for Christmas 1902.

DRO D/DLI 2/1/273(33)

INDIA

**48** Soldiers of the 1st Battalion DLI are presented with the Queen's South Africa medal by General Wolseley at Wellington Barracks in India on 1 May 1903.

DRO D/DLI 2/1/346

INDIA

**50** Captain Michael Goring-Jones, 1st Battalion DLI, poses with a man-eating tiger he shot during a hunting expedition in India in 1904.

DRO D/DLI 2/2/117(3)

**49** This is an informal portrait of Mess Sergeant McKenzie, 1st Battalion DLI, with his family and servants in India, about 1903.

DRO D/DLI 7/427/2(49)

**INDIA**

**51** Soldiers of the 2nd Battalion DLI, led by their Lieutenant, train
for the Evelyn Wood Competition at Aldershot, Hampshire, in 1904.
This competition tested both marching and shooting abilities.

HAMPSHIRE

**52** Bandsman Jimmy Durham with the Band of the 2nd Battalion
DLI at Corunna Barracks in Aldershot, Hampshire, in 1904.
Jimmy had enlisted in 1899 when aged about 14 years old.

**HAMPSHIRE**

**53** Part-time Volunteer soldiers from the 2nd Volunteer Battalion DLI on exercise during their annual camp, about 1905.

**NORTH EAST ENGLAND**

**54** Four Volunteers from the recently-formed "M"(Cyclists)
Company 1st Volunteer Battalion DLI at annual camp, about 1905.

DRO D/DLI 2/5/39(1)

**55** Part-time Volunteer soldiers of the 2nd Volunteer Battalion DLI filling mattresses with straw at the start of their annual camp, about 1905.

DRO D/DLI 2/6/10(169)

**56** Part-time Territorial soldiers of "C" Company 5th Battalion DLI cooking their dinners during their annual two-week camp, about 1910.

DRO D/DLI 2/5/57

NORTH EAST ENGLAND

Sunday Afternoon in Deerbolt Camp, 1910.

**57** A Sunday afternoon entertainment for the families of the
3rd (Militia) Battalion DLI at Deerbolt Camp, near Barnard Castle,
in 1910.

DRO D/DLI 2/3/46

COUNTY DURHAM

**58** This group from the 2nd Battalion DLI at Cork in Ireland, about 1908, includes two soldiers dressed and equipped for bayonet practice.

DRO D/DLI 2/2/195

IRELAND

**59** Here, soldiers of the 2nd Battalion DLI pose inside their sparsely-furnished room at Youghall Barracks, County Cork, Ireland, about 1908.

DRO D/DLI 7/498/33

**60** This portrait of Private James Francis Durham, 2nd Battalion DLI, was taken in Cork, Ireland, about 1909. Jimmy Durham died of pneumonia in August 1910, while stationed at Fermoy near Cork.

DRO D/DLI 7/194/9

IRELAND

**61** The 2nd Battalion DLI and Sherwood Foresters parade at Fermoy in Ireland, on 13 May 1910, to hear the proclamation of King George V.

DRO D/DLI 2/2/136(34)

IRELAND

**62** Led by their Band, the 4th (Militia) Battalion DLI marches down from Deerbolt Camp past the Deer Bolt Inn towards Barnard Castle, about 1911.

DRO D/DLI 2/4/384(1)

**63** New Colours are dedicated by the Reverend Henry Gee, before the Earl of Durham presents them to the 3rd Battalion DLI at Hartley Camp in Northumberland on 1 June 1912.

DRO D/DLI 2/3/51

# NORTH EAST ENGLAND

**64** In 1912, "H" Company 1st Battalion DLI set up camp at Khanspur on the North West Frontier of India.

DRO D/DLI 2/1/367

INDIA

MILITARY FUNERAL 3RD D.L.I. BARNARD CASTLE
DROWNING FATILITY TEES JUNE 15TH 1913

**65** On 15 June 1913, a military funeral was held at Barnard
Castle, County Durham, for Private Smith of the 3rd Battalion
DLI, who had drowned in the River Tees in a swimming accident.

DRO D/DLI 2/3/67(1)

COUNTY DURHAM

**67** The 6th Battalion DLI attends church parade, on Sunday 2 August 1914, during annual camp at Conway. This was the battalion's last church parade before the First World War began.

DRO D/DLI 2/6/10(207)

**66** Here, two young Territorial soldiers of the 9th Battalion DLI pose with the battalion's mascot during annual camp at Conway in North Wales in July 1914.

DRO D/DLI 7/805(155)

**68** After mobilization in August 1914, the 8th Battalion DLI moved into these tents at Ravensworth Castle, near Gateshead, County Durham, to train for war.

DRO D/DLI 2/8/11(65)

**69** Following Kitchener's call for Volunteers, recruits for the Durham Pals (18th Battalion DLI) parade on the Racecourse in Durham in September 1914 and are inspected by the Earl of Durham.

DRO D/DLI 2/18/25

**70** Just weeks after the start of the First World War, Durham Pals report for duty at Cocken Hall - the new Headquarters of the 18th Battalion DLI - near Durham, 1914.

DRO D/DLI 2/18/30

FIRST WORLD WAR

**71** Durham Pals from "C" Company 18th Battalion DLI stand outside Newton Hall, near Durham, in November 1914.

DRO D/DLI 2/18/29

**73** Durham Pals crowd inside a newly-built wooden barrack hut at Cocken Hall, near Durham, during the winter of 1914 - 1915.

DRO D/DLI 2/18/40

**72** A new recruit to the 18th Battalion DLI is fitted with his khaki uniform at Cocken Hall, near Durham, in late 1914.

DRO D/DLI 2/18/31

FIRST WORLD WAR

**74** Before real military training begins at Cocken Hall, the Durham Pals get fit during the winter of 1914 -1915, with long route marches and sports like football and boxing.

DRO D/DLI 2/18/36

FIRST WORLD WAR

**75** Four unknown Durham Pals display the new uniforms and equipment issued to the 18th Battalion DLI at Cocken Hall, near Durham, during the winter of 1914 - 1915.

DRO D/DLI 2/18/24(1)

FIRST WORLD WAR

Text on train: GOOD LUCK TO THE 17TH DLI BARNARD CASTLE SEP 24TH 1915 13

**76** Soldiers of the 17th (Reserve) Battalion DLI leave Barnard
Castle railway station, County Durham, on 24 September 1915.

DRO D/DLI 2/17/8

FIRST WORLD WAR

**77** Privates Jackson and Pattison from "D" Company 6th Battalion DLI in a trench at Shrapnel Corner, near Ypres in Belgium, in May 1915.

DRO D/DLI 2/6/10(316)

**78** Private Matthew Perry (left with biscuit) from Consett waits in a trench, near Ypres, in Belgium, for orders with other soldiers of "D" Company 6th Battalion DLI on 24 May 1915.

DRO D/DLI 2/6/10(317)

# FIRST WORLD WAR

**79** The same 6th Battalion DLI soldiers marching through Ypres, in Belgium, later that day (24 May 1915). Private Perry (front right) was killed by shellfire an hour after this photograph was taken.

DRO D/DLI 2/6/10(324)

**80** Captain Roland Bradford, 2nd Battalion DLI, at Armentières in France in 1915. In 1916, he was awarded the Victoria Cross. In 1917, he was killed in action.

DRO D/DLI 7/87/2(20)

**81** Second Lieutenant William Thompson (right), 9th Battalion DLI, with a group of other officers, somewhere in France in 1917.

DRO D/DLI 7/701/2(89)

# FIRST WORLD WAR

**82** A Prisoner of War Camp for Allied officers at Gutersloh in Westphalia, Germany, sometime in 1915.

DRO D/DLI 2/8/12(45)

**83** Captain Elliot Leybourne (seated second right), 8th Battalion DLI, with other prisoners in Gutersloh Prisoner of War Camp in Germany. He was wounded and captured near Ypres, Belgium, in April 1915.

DRO D/DLI 2/8/12(39)

**84** This is the 20th (Wearside) Battalion DLI's Cross Country
Running Team photographed with their trophy, sometime in 1915.

DRO D/DLI 7/805(62)

FIRST WORLD WAR

**85** A physical training display by soldiers of the 4th Battalion DLI outside their Headquarters at Seaham Harbour, County Durham, in 1918.

DRO D/DLI 7/35/1(55)

**86** Here soldiers of the 7th Battalion DLI arrive at Sunderland
Town Hall, on 20 June 1919, before their final demobilisation and
return to civilian life.

DRO D/DLI 2/7/18(10)

# FIRST WORLD WAR

**87** These young Soldiers from "B" and "D" Companies, 52nd Battalion DLI, formed part of the British Army of Occupation in Cologne, Germany, in 1919.

DRO D/DLI 7/805(110)

**88** In May 1919, the 1st Battalion DLI occupied this camp at Ali Musjid in the Khyber Pass during the Third Afghan War.

DRO D/DLI 2/1/383

INDIA

**89** This is the 2nd Battalion DLI's Dramatic Club at Ahmednagar, India, in December 1922. The cast of Gilbert and Sullivan's "Ruddigore" was composed of soldiers plus their wives and daughters.

DRO D/DLI 2/2/223

INDIA

MARRIED QUARTERS

SOLON, SIMLA HILLS. 1926. INDIA. 2 COYS 2ND DLI.

**90** Two companies of the 2nd Battalion DLI at Solon in the Simla Hills, India, parade in 1926. Above the parade ground on the hill are the battalion's married quarters.

**INDIA**

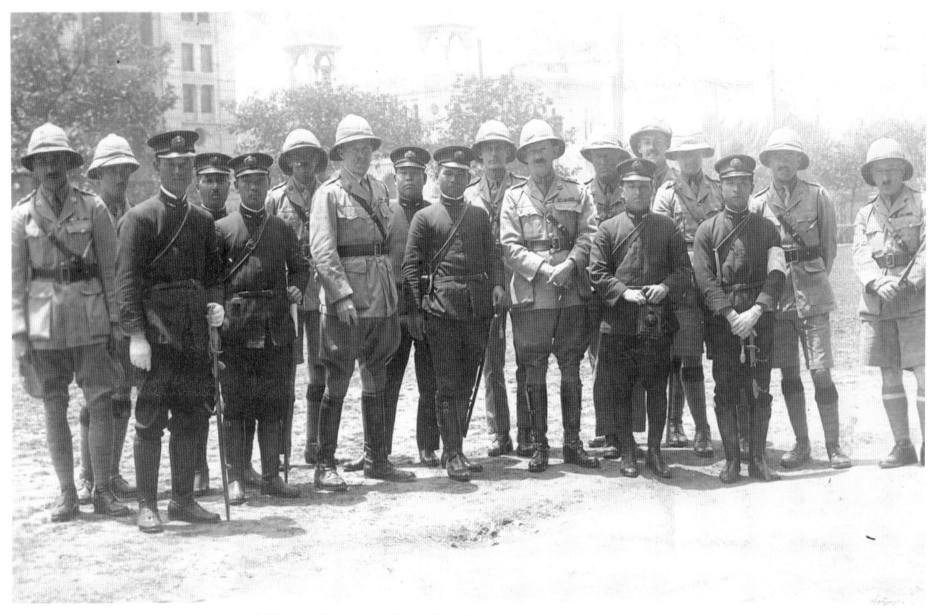

**91** Officers of the 2nd Battalion DLI pose with Japanese Marine officers at Shanghai in China, on 10 May 1927.

DRO D/DLI 2/2/243

CHINA

**92** The 1st Battalion DLI was stationed at Mustapha Barracks in Alexandria, Egypt, in 1928. This is the outside of the hairdressing saloon, which was also a photographic studio.

EGYPT

**93** Inside the hairdressing saloon at Mustapha Barracks in Alexandria, Egypt, in 1928, where there were separate entrances for officers and other ranks.

EGYPT

**94** Here King George V inspects a DLI Guard of Honour, from the Depot in Fenham at Jesmond Station, October 1928. The King was in Newcastle to open the new Tyne Bridge.

DRO D/DLI 1/5/21

NEWCASTLE UPON TYNE

**95** Razmak Camp high in the mountains on the North West Frontier of India was home to the 2nd Battalion DLI for a year from November 1929.

DRO D/DLI 7/618/8

**96** The 2nd Battalion DLI's machine guns firing near Razmak on the North West Frontier of India in 1930.

DRO D/DLI 7/449/1(22)

INDIA

**97** A patrol of the 2nd Battalion DLI near Razmak on the North West Frontier of India in 1930.

DRO D/DLI 2/2/145(115)

INDIA

**98** Lieutenant Abdy Ricketts, 2nd Battalion DLI, and his wife (extreme right) set off on a tiger shoot in India in February 1933.

DRO D/DLI 7/576/77

**99** Born in India of a military family, Abdy Ricketts joined the 2nd Battalion DLI in 1925. A keen horseman and polo player, he finally retired from the army as a Major General in 1957. This photograph show Ricketts in 1926.

DRO D/DLI 2/1/267 (35)

INDIA

**100** Here the Prince of Wales inspects a Guard of Honour by the 1st Battalion DLI during his visit to Middlesbrough, Yorkshire, in 1932.

DRO D/DLI 2/1/475

YORKSHIRE

**101** Men of the 1st Battalion DLI act as "Napoleonic" soldiers
during a performance at the Northern Command Tattoo at
Ravensworth Castle, near Gateshead, County Durham,
in July 1934.

DRO D/DLI 7/301/3(19)

**102** To mark the Royal Jubilee in May 1935 at Crook, County Durham, a parade was held at the War Memorial in the Market Square with "D" Company 6th Battalion DLI.

DRO D/DLI 2/6/178

COUNTY DURHAM

**103** Maps are checked at a roadside halt near St Albans, in Hertfordshire, during the 1st Battalion DLI's training drive, in May 1935, from Blackdown Camp in Hampshire to the Depot in Newcastle upon Tyne.

SOUTHERN ENGLAND

**104** "B" Company 1st Battalion DLI parades in its new role as a mechanised machine gun company at Blackdown Camp, Aldershot, Hampshire, in 1936.

DRO D/DLI 2/1/482

**HAMPSHIRE**

**105** Before leaving the Sudan for England, the 2nd Battalion
DLI held a final parade in October 1937 at the South Barracks
in Khartoum.

DRO D/DLI 2/2/276

SUDAN

106 Taken at Southampton in November 1937, these 2nd Battalion DLI veterans had been away from the UK on overseas service since 1919.

DRO D/DLI 2/2/279

**108** Soldiers of the 1st Battalion DLI play an ice hockey match at Tientsin Country Club in China during the winter of 1938 - 1939.

DRO D/DLI 2/1/280(111)

**107** A soldier of the 1st Battalion DLI stands sentry at Tientsin in China during the winter of 1938 - 1939.

DRO D/DLI 2/1/280(304)

**CHINA**

**109** Soldiers of the 1st Battalion DLI patrol down Racecourse Road during the flooding at Tientsin in China in August 1939.

DRO D/DLI 2/1/280(193)

**110** A game of sack football is played during the 1st Battalion DLI's Inkerman Day celebrations on 5 November 1939 in Hong Kong, China.

DRO D/DLI 2/1/280(277)

# CHINA

**111** Second Lieutenant Richard Annand VC (front left) outside Buckingham Palace on 3 September 1940 following the presentation of his Victoria Cross by King George VI.

DRO D/DLI 7/14/1

**112** A platoon of the 1st Battalion Durham Home Guard at Rowlands Gill, County Durham, about 1942.

DRO D/DLI 5/3/1/3

**113** Between July and December 1940, the 1st Battalion took up defensive positions in the North African desert at Mersa Matruh on the border between Egypt and Libya.

DRO D/DLI 2/1/518

**114** At Mersa Matruh, on the border between Egypt and Libya, in November 1940, the 1st Battalion DLI's Headquarters was set up in an old underground tomb. Here Captain and Adjutant "Oscar" Norman is using HQ's only telephone.

DRO D/DLI 2/1/280(374)

# SECOND WORLD WAR

**115** Major Mark Leather, 1st Battalion DLI, and Dorothy Hedges walk past the Guard of Honour following their marriage in Cairo in Egypt in 1942.

DRO D/DLI 2/1/280(340)

**116** Here prisoners, including Durhams, unpack Red Cross parcels at Stalag 20A Prisoner of War Camp at Thorn in Poland about 1941.

DRO D/DLI 7/767/34

**117** Here prisoners, including Durhams, sit on the roof of a hut in Stalag 20A Prisoner of War Camp at Thorn in Poland about 1941.

DRO D/DLI 7/767/35

SECOND WORLD WAR

**118** A prisoners' concert party performs on stage, probably at
Stalag 20A Prisoner of War Camp at Thorn in Poland about 1941.

SECOND WORLD WAR

**119** Somewhere in North Africa about 1942, a 3″ mortar crew of the 8th Battalion DLI prepares to open fire.

DRO D/DLI 7/762/1(49)

**120** Private Adam Wakenshaw VC, 9th Battalion DLI, is being reburied at El Alamein Cemetery in Egypt in 1943. He had gained his posthumous Victoria Cross in June 1942 at Mersa Matruh, on the border between Egypt and Libya.

DRO D/DLI 7/735/16

**121** Young soldiers of the 70th Battalion DLI train with a 6-pounder anti-tank gun at Westwick Camp, Barnard Castle, County Durham, about 1942.

DRO D/DLI 2/34/4(117)

**122** Prime Minister Winston Churchill visits the 70th (Young Soldiers) Battalion DLI at Westwick Camp, Barnard Castle, County Durham, on 4 December 1942.

DRO D/DLI 2/34/4(29)

SECOND WORLD WAR

**123** This bridge at Primosole, near Catania in Sicily, was the scene of fierce fighting in July 1943 between the 6th, 8th and 9th Battalions DLI and German paratroops.

DRO D/DLI 7/762/1(114)

**124** After the liberation of Sicily, soldiers of the 151st Brigade (6th, 8th and 9th Battalions DLI) relax at the seaside at Stazzo in August 1943.

DRO D/DLI 7/762/1(105)

SECOND WORLD WAR

**125** These are the lower slopes of Garrison Hill at Kohima in India in May 1944, where the 2nd Battalion DLI fought to halt the Japanese invasion of North East India.

DRO D/DLI 7/121/13(11)

SECOND WORLD WAR

**126** "New Gateshead" cemetery for the dead of the 2nd Battalion
DLI was created on Garrison Hill after the Battle of Kohima,
India, in May 1944.

DRO D/DLI 2/2/299(1)

**127** King George VI inspects the soldiers of the 151st Brigade (6th, 8th and 9th Battalions DLI) at Shudy Camp in Cambridgeshire on 23 February 1944.

DRO D/DLI 7/762/1(131)

**128** General Eisenhower inspects the soldiers of the 151st Brigade (6th, 8th and 9th Battalions DLI) on 13 May 1944 during the final preparations for D-Day.

DRO D/DLI 7/762/1(132)

**129** After D-Day, DLI soldiers advance during the Battle of Lingèvres near Tilley sur Seulles in Normandy in June 1944.

DRO D/DLI 2/6/11(603)

SECOND WORLD WAR

**130** On 10 June 1944, Sunderland, County Durham, conferred the "Freedom of the Borough" on the DLI. Here soldiers from the Depot parade with the Colours outside the Town Hall.

DRO D/DLI 1/13/5(2)

**131** In March 1945, during the advance in Burma, soldiers from "A" Company 2nd Battalion DLI rest on Pagoda Hill near Mandalay.

DRO D/DLI 7/121/13(26)

SECOND WORLD WAR

**132** In April 1945, only days before the end of the war, Captain Roy Griffiths (standing front right) poses with "D" Company's Headquarters, 9th Battalion DLI, at Nienberg near Bremen, Germany.

DRO D/DLI 7/273/15(10)

**133** Durham soldiers took part in the relief of Belsen Concentration Camp in Germany in May 1945. Here the huts are burned to prevent the spread of disease.

DRO D/DLI 7/404/28(22)

SECOND WORLD WAR

**134** On 7 September 1945, soldiers of the 9th Battalion DLI took part in the Victory Parade in Berlin, Germany, along with Russian and American forces.

DRO D/DLI 7/273/15(18)

SECOND WORLD WAR

**135** Field Marshal Montgomery with Major Ian English MC (third left) inspects a Guard of Honour from the 6th and 8th Battalions DLI at Huddersfield, Yorkshire, on 26 October 1945.

DRO D/DLI 2/8/174

YORKSHIRE

**136** "S" Company, 1st Battalion DLI, parades through Salonika, Greece, on 8 April 1948. In the lead Carrier is Corporal Henderson (driver) with Captain Fowle (standing) and Private Robertshaw (rear).

DRO D/DLI 2/1/280(479)

GREECE

**137** This parade was held at Brancepeth Castle, the Regiment's Depot near Durham City, on 25 September 1948 to mark the amalgamation of the 1st and 2nd Battalions DLI.

DRO D/DLI 2/1/280(501)

COUNTY DURHAM

**138** Company Sergeant Loyn (centre) with children at a
Christmas Party held on 26 December 1949 at "C" Company 6th
Battalion DLI's Drill Hall at Spennymoor, County Durham.

DRO D/DLI 2/6/11(735)

COUNTY DURHAM

**139** Bugle Major Albert Shippen leads the Band and Bugles up Owengate in Durham City on 9 July 1950 for the laying-up of the 1st and 2nd Battalion DLI's Colours.

DRO D/DLI 2/1/280(607)

**140** The 1st and 2nd Battalion DLI's Colours are paraded for the last time on Palace Green before being laid-up in Durham Cathedral on 9 July 1950.

DRO D/DLI 2/1/288(92)

**141** Here the Bishop of Durham dedicates the DLI's Memorial Garden at Durham Cathedral, after the laying-up of the Colours on 9 July 1950.

DRO D/DLI 2/1/288(67)

# COUNTY DURHAM

**142** On 25 September 1952, Field Marshal Slim (left), during his visit to the 2nd Battalion DLI at Deerbolt Camp near Barnard Castle, County Durham, talks to Private Harry Ovington.

DRO D/DLI 2/2/148(13)

**143** Following the battalion's arrival at Pusan in Korea in September 1952, soldiers of the 1st Battalion DLI throw sweets to local children.

DRO D/DLI 2/1/20(22)

**144** "Little Gibraltar" was a front-line hill in Korea occupied in 1953 by the 1st Battalion DLI. Anyone who ignored the warning risked wounding or death from mortar or artillery fire.

DRO D/DLI 2/1/541

**KOREA**

**145** Privates Milburn (left) and Evans (right) of "C" Company 1st Battalion DLI in 1953 with one of the South Korean soldiers attached to the Durhams during the Korean War.

DRO D/DLI 2/1/21(4)

**146** The Roman Catholic chaplain, Father Petrie, says an open-air mass for soldiers of the 1st Battalion DLI in Korea in 1953.

DRO D/DLI 2/1/20(338)

KOREA

**147** These Buglers of the 1st Battalion DLI took part in the unveiling of the El Alamein Memorial in Egypt on 24 October 1954.

DRO D/DLI 2/1/280(686)

**EGYPT**

**148** Mrs Gwen Harris and Lieutenant Colonel Mark Leather, Commanding Officer, 2nd Battalion DLI, at a fancy dress party in the officers' mess at Wuppertal in Germany on 6 January 1955.

DRO D/DLI 2/2/148(199)

**149** The 2nd Battalion DLI won the Army Football Cup at Aldershot Military Stadium, Hampshire, on 27 April 1955. The captain (with cup) was Corporal Allison, a professional footballer with Blyth Spartans.

DRO D/DLI 2/2/148(274)

**150** Following its disbanding, the 2nd Battalion DLI parades through the Market Place in Durham for the last time on 10 July 1955.

DRO D/DLI 2/2/148(378)

COUNTY DURHAM

**151** Sergeant George Iceton MM (standing centre) with the 6th Battalion DLI's Machine Gun Team at the Drill Hall in Barnard Castle, County Durham, in May 1957.

DRO D/DLI 2/6/12(179)

COUNTY DURHAM

**152** Soldiers of the 6th Battalion DLI at the Unveiling of the War Memorial at Shildon, County Durham, on 2 June 1957.

DRO D/DLI 2/6/12(204)

COUNTY DURHAM

**153** Queen Elizabeth II inspects a Guard of Honour of the 6th
Battalion DLI at Newton Aycliffe, County Durham, on 27 May 1960.

DRO D/DLI 2/6/12(375)

COUNTY DURHAM

**155** The Duke of Edinburgh, with Major Mulhall (centre), inspects a Guard of Honour of the 8th Battalion DLI at the opening of County Hall, Durham, on 14 October 1963.

DRO D/DLI 2/1/289(126)

**154** Major General Lord Thurlow (centre), Commanding 50th (Northumbrian) Division, talking with two miners, both Territorials with the 6th Battalion DLI, at Chilton Colliery, County Durham, on 26 May 1961.

DRO D/DLI 2/6/12(462)

# COUNTY DURHAM

**156** Here soldiers of the 1st Battalion DLI enjoy a traditional Christmas dinner in Hong Kong, China, in 1963 despite the warm weather.

DRO D/DLI 2/1/287(73)

**157** Wives of the Sergeants of the 1st Battalion DLI formed their own "Ladies' Club" when the battalion was stationed in Gun Club Barracks at Kowloon, Hong Kong, China, in 1964.

DRO D/DLI 2/1/712

**159** Privates Bond, Stratton, Wetheral, Hoey, Dodd, Tweddle, Constable and Traynor (left to right), all Regulars with the 1st Battalion DLI, enjoy a quiet drink in Hong Kong, China, in 1965.

DRO D/DLI 2/1/289(37)

**158** "Johnny and the Dingo's" were just one of the many "beat" groups that formed whilst the 1st Battalion DLI was based in Hong Kong, China, in 1964 - 1965.

DRO D/DLI 7/534/13(77)

CHINA

**160** Sergeant Parker (left front) returns from patrol to Nibong, "C" Company 1st Battalion DLI's fortified base in Borneo in 1966.

DRO D/DLI 2/1/728

**161** Major Michael McBain (standing left with rifle but without shirt) commanded "C" Company 1st Battalion DLI at Nibong in Borneo in 1966.

DRO D/DLI 2/1/287(364)

**BORNEO**

**162** Privates Emery, Sanderson, Dunn, Bond, Patterson, Ludlow and Adamson (left to right) play dominoes at Nibong, "C" Company 1st Battalion DLI's base in Borneo, in 1966.

DRO D/DLI 2/1/735

BORNEO

Last camp it might be, but the Safety Boat crew looks happy enough. Standing by in case of landing assault craft trouble

**163** River crossing during the Battle Efficiency Competition at the 6th Battalion DLI's last annual camp at Bodney in Norfolk in May 1966.

DRO D/DLI 2/6/12(755)

**164** Brigadier Peter Jeffreys (centre), the 6th Battalion DLI's Honorary Colonel, visits the battalion's last annual camp at Bodney in Norfolk in May 1966.

DRO D/DLI 2/6/12(775)

**165** The 1st Battalion DLI "double past" as they troop the Colours on the parade ground at Colchester, Essex, on 6 April 1968. This march was at 140 paces to the minute.

DRO D/DLI 2/1/289(116)

**ESSEX**

**166** Private Alan Clews, 1st Battalion DLI, on observation duty with the United Nations peacekeeping force near Limassol in Cyprus between May and October 1968.

CYPRUS

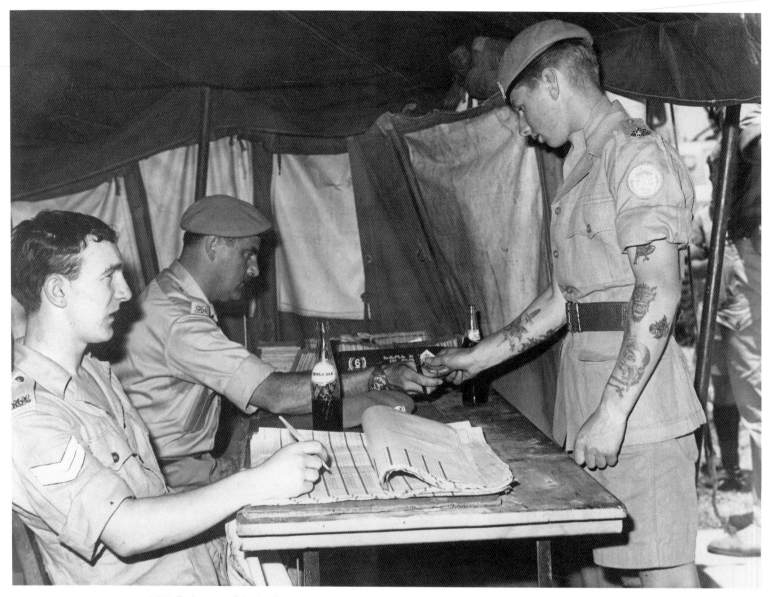

**167** Private Chris Lawton of the 1st Battalion receives his pay whilst serving with the United Nations at Limassol in Cyprus between May and October 1968.

DRO D/DLI 2/1/289(99)

CYPRUS

**168** On 12 December 1968, Princess Alexandra, the last Colonel in Chief of The Durham Light Infantry, attends the final parade on Palace Green, as the Colours are laid-up in Durham Cathedral.

DRO D/DLI Acc: 2913(D) Vol. 9 (temp)

**169** Princess Alexandra inspects the DLI Association on Palace Green, Durham Cathedral, on 12 December 1968 before the final laying-up of the Colours of the 1st Battalion DLI.

DRO D/DLI 2/1/289(129)

COUNTY DURHAM

# Image of the
# SOLDIER

The very first photographs of the Regiment were probably taken in 1855 during the Crimean War and, over the next hundred years, tens of thousands more would be taken of the Durhams - in peace and in war - culminating in the final parade at Durham Cathedral in 1968.

These photographs are of all members of the Regimental family from the Regulars (full-time professional soldiers) who fought in every campaign from the Crimea to Borneo, to the part-time volunteer soldiers like the Militiamen, Rifle Volunteers and Territorials; and from the volunteers who joined Kitchener's New Army in 1914 to the National Servicemen who served after 1945.

First raised in 1758, the 68th Regiment of Foot was re-formed as a Light Infantry regiment in 1808. In 1881 it became the 1st Battalion The Durham Light Infantry. The first photographs of these Regular soldiers were probably taken during the Crimean War, 1854 - 1856, when the 68th Light Infantry joined the British and French invasion of the Crimea to capture Russia's naval base at Sebastopol [Photos 1-4]. At Inkerman, on 5 November 1854, the Durhams played a major part in the most important battle of the war, in spite of fighting in uniforms, more at home on the parade ground than the battlefield. During the bitter winter that followed, cold, wet and disease killed

more British soldiers than enemy bullets, before new warm clothing arrived in the spring of 1855. In May 1855, Russian soldiers attacked the Durham's trenches. After the action, Private John Byrne, who had already rescued a wounded soldier at Inkerman, and Captain Thomas de Courcy Hamilton, were awarded the Victoria Cross - the first awarded to the Regiment. With the war finally won, the Durhams left the Crimea in May 1856.

Meanwhile in County Durham, just before the start of the Crimean War, the old Militia - originally set up in 1759 as a home defence force - was revived and then divided into the 1st South Durham Militia based at Barnard Castle [Photo 5] and the 2nd North Durham Militia based in Durham. When the Crimean War began, these two Regiments were embodied (called up) at home, with the Militiamen serving as full-time soldiers, until the danger had passed.

In 1858, after just a few months in England, the 68th Light Infantry sailed for Burma, which had only recently been added to the British Empire. During five long years on garrison duty, the Durhams amused themselves with hunting, vegetable growing, amateur theatricals and sport, especially cricket [Photos 6-7].

Back home, fear of war with France and the threat of invasion, forced the British government to allow home defence units to form - the Volunteers. In County Durham, between 1859 and 1861, nineteen Rifle Volunteer corps were raised, including the 3rd at Sunderland

and the 4th at Bishop Auckland [Photos 8-9]. These early Volunteers were organised like clubs, with members paying an annual subscription. Although the government supplied the rifles, the Volunteers and their supporters had to buy the uniforms, equipment, stores and drill halls.

In January 1864, the 68th Light Infantry, including many veterans of the Crimean War, landed in New Zealand, where the Maoris had gone to war to try to halt the spread of the British settlements on North Island [Photos 11-14]. In April 1864, a British force attacked Gate Pah (a Maori fort). The attack failed and the British were driven off with heavy losses. In June the British discovered the Maoris building a new pah at Te Ranga and stormed the unfinished defences. This was the last major battle fought by the Durhams in New Zealand.

The soldiers of the 68th Light Infantry were, however, not the only Regular ancestors of the DLI. Originally part of the East India Company's Army, the 106th Light Infantry [Photo 15] was formed in 1862 and, though this Regiment had no historic link with County Durham, it became the 2nd Battalion The Durham Light Infantry in 1881.

During the 1860s and 1870s, the North and South Durham Militias [Photos 10, 16-19], in spite of competition from the new Rifle Volunteers, continued to train to defend their County in time of war. Most of these Militiamen were part-time soldiers who only attended the annual

training but each Regiment also had a Permanent Staff of ex-Regulars. In 1868, the South Durham Militia became Fusiliers and adopted a new uniform - the only English Militia Regiment to be made into Fusiliers.

With the end of the New Zealand War, the last fought by the 68th Light Infantry, the Regiment settled into routine garrison duties at home or in India [Photos 20-22]. And, once again, cricket became a major occupation.

In 1881, as part of major changes to the British Army, the 68th and 106th Light Infantry Regiments were joined together to form the 1st and 2nd Battalions The Durham Light Infantry, with one battalion always based at home while the other served overseas [Photos 23-24]. This change was not welcomed, and it was many years before the old 68th and 106th names stopped being used.

The 1881 Army changes also affected the Militia, with the South and North Durham Militias becoming the 3rd and 4th Battalions DLI. In 1885, during a war scare over Afghanistan, the newly-named 3rd Battalion DLI was embodied and left Barnard Castle for Colchester [Photos 25-30]. Little happened during this time, except for a fight between the Durham soldiers and local "toughs".

The invasion of Egypt from the Sudan in 1885, led to the 2nd Battalion DLI gaining the DLI's first battle honour. The battalion was at Gibraltar when it was ordered to join an Army in Egypt. Finally moving south after months of inactivity, this combined British and Egyptian Army met and defeated the Sudanese invaders on 30 December 1885 at Ginnis on the banks of the River Nile. After the battle, a patrol of Mounted Infantry led by a young DLI officer, Henry de Lisle, found a Sudanese child abandoned by the river [Photo 31]. Adopted by the 2nd Battalion's Sergeants and taken to India in 1887, this boy, known as Jimmy Durham, eventually joined the Regiment.

The 2nd Battalion DLI remained in India until 1902 [Photos 32-34]. During these years, Henry de Lisle captained a polo team that was the best in India, beating all rivals, including the cavalry, and winning every major trophy. However, there was more to service in India than sport; training was hard, the climate was often unhealthy and disease in the crowded cities was ever present.

Meanwhile at home the Militiamen continued their training, while the Regulars of the 1st Battalion entertained the Crown Prince of Siam at Aldershot, little realising that they would soon be off to war [Photos 35-36].

During the Boer War, 1899 to 1902, all sections of The Durham Light Infantry - Regulars, Militiamen and Volunteers - were in action together for the first and only time [Photos 37-44]. In 1899, the 1st Battalion left Aldershot to join the Army in Natal. At Vaal Krantz on 5 February 1900, the Durhams crossed the Tugela River hoping to break the Boer defences and relieve the besieged town of Ladysmith, but the attack failed and casualties were heavy. After the Relief of Ladysmith, these Regulars spent the rest of the war on guard duties. Though based in India, the 2nd Battalion sent Mounted Infantry to South Africa in 1900, where they fought with distinction at Sanna's Post and in many other minor actions. During the war, the Militia was embodied and both the 3rd and 4th Battalions volunteered for service in South Africa. However, neither saw much action, spending their days instead on convoy duty or in blockhouses guarding bridges and railway lines. Finally, the Volunteers sent over four hundred men to serve as reinforcements with the Regulars. As in all previous wars, more Durhams died during the Boer War from disease than in battle, with casualties of one hundred dead and one hundred and fifty wounded.

In 1902, at the end of the Boer War, the 1st Battalion DLI sailed from South Africa to India, replacing the 2nd Battalion at Wellington Barracks and, for the first time in their history, the two battalions met [Photos 45-50]. Astonishingly the 1st Battalion did not leave India and return home until 1919.

Back in England, the 2nd Battalion DLI settled into a new life [Photos 51-52]. Training was now focussed on musketry skills - a lesson hard-learnt from the Boer riflemen in South Africa - but there was still time for the older military traditions.

The Volunteers too learnt the lessons of the Boer War; training increased and the two-week annual camp allowed the part-time soldiers to experience life in the field. In 1908, another major Army reform saw the old Volunteers become Territorials, with the five Volunteer Battalions renamed the 5th, 6th, 7th, 8th and 9th Battalions DLI. At the same time, the old Durham Militia was changed again, becoming a new Special Reserve that would send reinforcements to the Regular battalions in time of war, but that still has time for less warlike pursuits [Photos 53-57].

In 1905, the 2nd Battalion DLI moved to Ireland, serving first at Cork and later at Fermoy [Photos 58-61]. Living conditions in these Irish barracks rooms were sparse and the cold and damp of Fermoy claimed the life of one famous soldier - Jimmy Durham.

The years before 1914 saw the Durhams, at home and in India, following the routines of peacetime training and ceremonial duties, unaware of the horrors that would soon overwhelm them [Photos 62-65]. In July 1914, the Durham Territorials went on their annual camp to North Wales. On 3 August, they were ordered back to Durham and then under canvas at Ravensworth Castle [Photos 66-68]. The First World War had begun.

In August 1914, there were only nine DLI battalions. By November 1918, the DLI had grown to forty-three battalions, twenty-two of which saw action overseas. In the first months of war, thousands of Durham men heard Lord Kitchener's call for volunteers - "Your Country Needs You" - and left their civilian jobs to join a New Army. These volunteers formed into Service Battalions like the "Durham Pals" - 18th Battalion DLI - and began the long months of training to prepare them for war [Photos 69-75,84].

During the First World War, DLI battalions fought on the Western Front in Belgium and France at Ypres, Loos, Somme, Arras, Messines, Passchendale, Cambrai, in the German attacks of 1918, and in the final advances that led to victory in 1918. Other Durham battalions fought in Egypt, Italy and Salonika, while the old Militia guarded the Durham coastline from German attack [Photos 76-81,85].

From the first, casualties were heavy. On the River Aisne in September 1914, the 2nd Battalion lost in one day's fighting as many men as the entire Regiment had lost in the Boer War. At Ypres in 1915, the Durham Territorials lost a third of their strength killed or wounded just days after landing in France. And on the Somme, on 1 July 1916, the Durham Pals lost over half their strength killed or wounded. The First World War cost the DLI thirteen thousand men killed, dead from wounds or disease, and thousands more wounded or gassed. Many others were taken prisoner and spent years in camps where, as the war continued, conditions got worse [Photos 82-83].

In 1919 with the war won, most of the Durhams were demobilised and returned to their civilian lives, though some were briefly sent into Germany as part of the Army of Occupation [Photos 86-87].

While in India, the 1st Battalion DLI, having spent the entire First World War on the North West Frontier, took part in the short-lived Third Afghan War of 1919 before finally returning home [Photo 88].

For the Regular soldiers, and especially the officers, the end of the First World War meant a return to "real soldiering" - as it was called - and the familiar routines of garrison life, training, ceremonials, sport and the occasional brief action in defence of the Empire. Before 1914 only one Regular battalion had been abroad in any year, after 1919 new commitments sent both overseas.

In 1920, the 2nd Battalion DLI arrived in India [Photos 91-93], and later served in China [Photo 91]. In 1927 the 1st Battalion moved to Egypt and Alexandria [Photos 92-93]. Meanwhile in Durham, poverty and unemployment meant that there was no shortage of young recruits at the Depot in Newcastle upon Tyne [Photo 94].

Trouble on the North West Frontier of India saw the 2nd Battalion DLI sent, unaccompanied by their wives and families, to the camp at Razmak high in the mountains and, in one action against local Mahsud tribesmen, Corporal Brooks won the only Military Medal awarded in 1930 [Photos 95-97]. Life in India for the Regulars soon returned to more usual pursuits [Photos 98-99].

In 1930, the 1st Battalion DLI returned home and was posted to Catterick Camp in North Yorkshire, close enough to allow it to take part for the first time in ceremonials and events in County Durham [Photos 100-101]. Meanwhile the DLI's Territorials, reformed in the 1920s, continued to play an important role in the life of the County [Photo 102].

The 1st Battalion moved south to Blackdown Camp at Aldershot in late 1934 and trained for two years as an experimental mechanised infantry unit with tracked carriers, lorries and motorbikes, before being ordered overseas to China in 1937 [Photos 103-104].

That same year, 1937, a small group of Regulars returned home, for the first time since 1919, after service with the 2nd Battalion DLI in Turkey, India, China and the Sudan [Photos 105-106]. The 2nd Battalion was still based at home when the Second World War began in 1939.

The 1st Battalion DLI landed in Shanghai in November 1937, where fighting between Chinese and invading Japanese forces threatened the International Settlement. In October 1938, the Durhams moved to Tientsin, where the bitterly cold winter, followed by summer floods, made life interesting [Photos 107-109]. The 1st Battalion DLI was still serving in China when the Second World War began [Photo 110].

During the Second World War, only eight DLI battalions saw action overseas - 1st, 2nd, 6th, 8th, 9th, 10th, 11th and 16th Battalions DLI - and three thousand Durhams were killed, with thousands more wounded or taken prisoner.

The 2nd Battalion's Regulars were the first in action on the River Dyle in Belgium in May 1940, when Second Lieutenant Richard Annand won the first Army Victoria Cross of the Second World War [Photo 111]. Later that summer, the Durham Home Guard was formed. Soon these volunteers were proudly wearing the DLI's cap badge, as they prepared to defend their County from invasion [Photo 112].

Following the retreat from Dunkirk, the action moved to North Africa, where the 1st Battalion's Regulars dug in to defend Egypt from invasion by the Italian Army [Photos 113-114]. But even in war, normal life continued as best it could [Photo 115].

Over three thousand Durhams were taken prisoner during the Second World War, the first at Dunkirk, then many others in North Africa. In the early years, conditions in the prison camps were not harsh, but by 1944, food shortages and other deprivations made life very miserable for the prisoners [Photos 116-118].

In North Africa in 1942, the DLI's Territorial battalions suffered initial defeats and were forced to retreat. During one defeat at Mersa Matruh in June, Private Adam Wakenshaw of the 9th Battalion DLI was awarded the Victoria Cross - the last awarded to the DLI. In October at El Alamein, these Durhams took their revenge, as part of General Montgomery's Eighth Army, and helped drive the German and Italian forces out of North Africa. [Photos 119-120].

Meanwhile in County Durham, some of the finest young soldiers in the British Army completed their training with the 70th Battalion before they too were sent overseas [Photos 121-122].

In 1943, following the victory in North Africa, the DLI's Territorial battalions took part in the invasion of Sicily and fought a fierce battle with German paratroops at Primosole Bridge [Photos 123-124].

In the Far East, between 1943 and 1945, the 2nd Battalion was the only Durham battalion to fight against the Japanese Army in India and Burma. These Durhams fought in the savage battle at Kohima in 1944 to halt the Japanese invasion of India [Photos 125-126].

After the fall of Sicily, the 6th, 8th and 9th Battalions DLI returned to Britain to train for D-Day. As part of the 50th Division, they landed on the beaches of Normandy in France on 6 June 1944 [Photos 127-129].

By 1945, victory was finally in sight. In the Far East, the 2nd Battalion took part in the long advance out of India and down into Burma. Meanwhile in Europe, some Durhams took part in the relief of Belsen concentration camp, while the 9th Battalion joined the final advance into Nazi Germany that led to the Allies' victory parade in Berlin [Photos 131-135].

With the end of the Second World War, the last chapter of The Durham Light Infantry's story began. At first, the Regulars returned to their familiar routines, with the 1st Battalion in Greece and the 2nd in the Far East. But the British Army was changing, manpower was short, and in 1948, the two Regular battalions merged into one. However recruiting to the DLI remained strong, and the 2nd Battalion was reborn in 1952. Meanwhile, the Territorials re-formed in County Durham but it was not long before the 9th Battalion became part of the Parachute Regiment, leaving only the 6th and 8th Battalions DLI to wear the cap badge **[Photos 136-142]**.

In September 1952, the 1st Battalion DLI landed at Pusan to serve with the United Nations in the Korean War. Almost half of these Durhams were young conscripts doing their National Service. Despite his fears that they would not be tough enough, Lieutenant Colonel Jeffreys, their Commanding Officer, later described them as "mature, self-reliant, imperturbable" fighting men. There were no major battles in the hills north of the River Imjin but the Durhams suffered over one hundred casualties in conditions very like those in the trenches during the First World War **[Photos 143-146]**.

As the British Empire weakened during the 1950s, the Regulars of the 1st Battalion DLI, bolstered by National Servicemen, served in "trouble spots" in Suez, Aden and Cyprus. The 2nd Battalion enjoyed a brief existence with the British Army of the Rhine at Wuppertal, before it was disbanded for the final time in 1955 **[Photos 147-150]**.

Back home, the 6th and 8th Battalion's Territorials continued to train and play their part in the life of the County, but changes were on the way **[Photos 151-155]**.

In 1963, the Regulars of the 1st Battalion DLI moved to Hong Kong with their families. Tension was high in the Colony, but there was still time for the Durhams to relax **[Photos 156-159]**.

While based in Hong Kong, the 1st Battalion DLI was ordered in 1966 to Borneo to battle against invading forces from Indonesia but the island's mountains and jungles proved a more unpleasant enemy. Operating from fortified bases, like Camp Nibong, the Durhams took the fight to their enemy and in one ambush Thomas Griffiths died - the last Durham Light Infantryman to be killed in action. After two hundred years, the DLI had fought its last battle **[Photos 160-162]**.

The same year, the DLI's Territorial battalions held their last camps. Early in 1967, the 6th and 8th Battalions merged to form the 6th/8th Battalion DLI, but this new battalion, too, was soon disbanded as a new Regiment - The Light Infantry - was born **[Photos 163-164]**.

The 1st Battalion DLI was at Colchester and preparing for the end, when it was ordered to join the United Nations' force on Cyprus in May 1968. All knew that the Durhams would soon become the 4th Battalion The Light Infantry and that the Battalion would be finally disbanded in 1969 **[Photos 165-167]**.

In December 1968, the new 4th Battalion The Light Infantry paraded before Princess Alexandra, the last Colonel in Chief of The Durham Light Infantry, and then laid-up the old Colours of the 1st Battalion DLI in Durham Cathedral. In March 1969, this new battalion was itself disbanded and its soldiers absorbed by the remaining three Light Infantry battalions. After 200 years of history, The Durham Light Infantry was no more **[Photos 168-169]**.

# BACKGROUND TO THE IMAGE OF THE SOLDIER PROJECT

The publication of this volume coincides with the completion of the project The Image of the Soldier, described below. In May, 1998, the Management Trustees of the Durham Light Infantry Charitable Funds agreed to the transfer of the records previously held in the Durham Light Infantry Museum at Aykley Heads to the Durham County Record Office in County Hall, also at Aykley Heads. The transfer of the records began in July of the same year.

Between 1998 and 2001 225 boxes of papers, volumes, photograph albums and loose photographs were received in the County Record Office as part of the Durham Light Infantry Collection.

All the DLI records transferred from the Museum, and received directly from individuals and the DLI Office, are given the reference D/DLI and remain the property of the Trustees, with whom the Record Office works closely.

Detailed descriptions of the records began to be produced as soon as they had been received in the Record Office.

Between July 1998 and December 2003, when the detailed catalogue was completed, a qualified archivist was working full-time on the records. The catalogue was word-processed by a member of staff specially recruited for the task for a year. This member of staff was financed by the Trustees of the DLI

The detailed catalogue has been available in paper form in 6 lever-arch files in the Office's searchroom since 1 January 2004. At the same time, the catalogue was incorporated into the Office's electronic database of all its catalogues which is available on its website. The database is searchable by any key word anywhere in the world. For example, somebody in Hong Kong may see how many references to that former colony are to be found in the records of the DLI (There are many).

The DLI collection includes records of the regiment, of the battalions, of the Home Guard, and records of individual soldiers. It also includes 30,000 photographs both in 216 albums and as loose photographs.

The photographs are of outstanding quality and interest and range in time from photographs of soldiers in Crimea in 1856 to photographs of the last parade of DLI soldiers on Palace Green, Durham in 1968. They are one of the most frequently consulted parts of the collection and are also frequently copied. Photographs are vulnerable and easily damaged by over-handling and over-copying and because the photographs had been listed and described in detail and those descriptions had been made available to the family and military historians all over the world, it was inevitable that demand to handle and copy the photographs would increase. To allow everybody to see and obtain copies of the photographs, the Image of the Soldier project is designed to produce a digital copy of every photograph whether it is in an album or on its own. The digital copy is attached to its description on the Office's database. 30,000 photographs have been scanned and the contents of 216 albums have been described in detail. To do this, the Heritage Lottery Fund provided finance from the Your Heritage strand of the Fund. From May 2005, all the photographs of the DLI transferred to the Record Office between 1998 and 2001 will be viewable on the Record Office's website, attached to a description on the Office's database.

The photographs may be seen throughout the world - it is no longer necessary to visit Durham to see them. Copies can be made without damaging the original photographs and this wonderful collection of images will be shown to the widest possible audience. The Office's website address is: www.durham.gov.uk/recordoffice

The Record Office must thank especially the Trustees of the DLI and the Heritage Lottery Fund for their support in making this unrivalled collection known to the world.

Supported by the Heritage Lottery Fund

# INDEX TO NAMES AND PLACES